LONDON, NEW YORK, MUNICH,
MELBOURNE, and DELHI

Designer and Photoshoot Director Lisa Lanzarini
Editor Julia March
Consultant Jane Hackett
Publishing Manager Mary Atkinson
Art Director Mark Richards
Production Nicola Torode, Erica Rosen

First published in Great Britain in 2003
This paperback edition first published in 2007 by
Dorling Kindersley Limited,
80 Strand, London WC2R 0RL

2 4 6 8 10 9 7 5 3 1
MD051 – 04/07

A CIP catalogue record for this book is available from the British Library.

ISBN 978-1-40532-637-7

Reproduced by Media Development and Printing, Ltd
Printed and bound by Toppan, China

discover more at
www.dk.com

I Love Ballet

Learn how to dance with the
CENTRAL SCHOOL OF BALLET

Written by Naia Bray-Moffatt
Photography by David Handley

Contents

Introduction

Almost as soon as we can walk, we love
to dance. This book tells you all about how
to learn a special kind of dance called ballet.
It's a fun and exciting activity. It can be for girls
and boys. You'll make new friends and enter a
whole world of magical movement.

Getting Ready

The first thing that Jamie has to do when she arrives at school with her dad is to sign in at reception so that the school knows she has arrived.

This is Jamie's first day at ballet school. She's a bit nervous but she's been looking forward to it for a long time and has got everything ready she will need for her lessons. You don't need much: a hairbrush and ribbon to tie long hair back, and special clothes and shoes for dancing in. Most of the time in class Jamie will wear a leotard that is easy to move in and which makes it easy for her teacher to see what she is doing.

Getting changed

In the changing rooms, Jamie meets another new girl, Jennifer. Jamie's pleased to make a new friend and they help each other get changed into their practice clothes. Soon they will be ready to start their first class.

Keeping neat and tidy

It's important for dancers to look neat and tidy. Jamie helps Jennifer tie back her long hair so that it doesn't fall in her eyes or her face when she is dancing and she can see what she is doing.

Ballet clothes

Jamie brings all the clothes she needs in a ballet bag. For practice, she will wear a stretchy pink leotard and soft pink shoes. A special net tutu may be worn for performances.

Ballet shoes, made of leather, canvas or satin, are soft to allow you to stretch your feet.

Arriving at the Class

The ballet class takes place in a large room called a studio which has lots of space for Jamie and the children to run and leap and turn. There are full-length mirrors on one wall to check your positions and a special wooden floor which springs a little when you jump so that it is not so hard on your feet. Wooden rails, called the *barre*, are attached to the walls.

Anna is a qualified teacher who learnt to dance at ballet school. She helps the children find the right way to do things.

Anna takes the register and welcomes everyone to the class.

The barre

Wooden rails around the walls are called the *barre*. These are for you to hold onto while you practise your ballet exercises.

The mirror   *The piano*

Music

Dancers learn to move in time to music and to express the mood of the music through their movements. In Jamie's class a pianist will play the piano to dance to.

Jamie practises a curtsey.

11

Warm-Up

To begin their warm-up exercises, the children sit in a circle with their legs stretched out in front of them. Alex finds it hard to keep his legs straight and Anna helps him stretch his knees.

Ballet classes always begin with gentle exercises to warm up and train the muscles in every part of your body. This is very important because otherwise you could hurt yourself and not be able to dance properly. This part of the class can be quiet and slow and will help you think hard about the new things you are learning.

Learning to sit up

This exercise warms up the fingers and arms

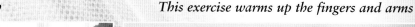

1 Head up

2 Head down

Putting the crown on

To help the children sit up properly Anna tells them to pretend they are putting a crown on and wearing fine jewels around their neck that they want to show off.

Coco lifts her head up to see if she can see the spider on the ceiling.

Head up, head down

To warm up the neck-muscles Anna asks the children to lift their heads and look up to the ceiling and see if they can spy an imaginary spider and then follow it as it lowers itself down to the floor.

Posture

Learning how to sit and stand correctly, with your head up and your back straight, is one of the first things you will be taught. It will help your balance and make you look like a proper dancer.

April sits up as tall as she can and tries to remember to hold her tummy in.

Putting her hands on her shoulders helps April keep her shoulders down and stand with a straight back.

April is standing incorrectly here, with a curved back. Anna calls it a banana back.

Flexing and stretching your feet warm up the muscles in your legs and feet.

Bending and Stretching

Dancers need to be able to move their bodies in lots of different ways and these bending and stretching exercises help your body become supple and flexible. The exercises should always be done slowly to properly stretch and warm your muscles. Doing the exercises sitting down helps Jamie and the class concentrate on their upper body.

Frog legs
With feet together to make a diamond shape and sitting up tall, April gently pushes down her knees to stretch her inside thigh muscles.

Sideways bends
Now it's time to bend and stretch from side to side. April is pretending her arms are the branches of a tree swaying in the wind. First the wind blows her "arm branches" over to the right and then to the left.

It's really hard to bend forward and keep your knees straight at the same time. The girls have to hold the stretch without bending their knees for 20 seconds before they sit up straight again.

Bending forwards

The pupils walk their hands down their legs until they reach their feet and "wake up" their toes. As they do this, they are bending their backs further and further forward.

Ballet Positions

April, Jamie and Coco stand with their feet in first, second and third positions. Fourth and fifth position are more difficult and they will learn these later on.

After they have warmed up, the class are ready to practise the five basic positions. They need to know how to hold their arms and feet in each position because many of the ballet steps they'll learn later on are based on these poses. They learn the arm positions first and then the feet, before putting them together.

1 In first position, hold your arms out in front in a gently curving shape and stand with heels together. Turn your feet and legs out as wide as they can go.

2 In second position, move your arms out to the side, keeping your elbows bent a little bit and hands curved. Stand with your heels about one foot's length apart and toes turned out.

3 Keep one arm out to the side and move the other in front of your body in third position. Remember to keep the hands curved. To stand, move one foot halfway in front of the other.

1st position

2nd position

3rd position

> *I can do the fifth position with my arms but I haven't learnt how to do it with my feet yet.*
>
> Jamie

It can be tricky to learn how to make shapes with your arms while your legs are doing different steps.

4 In fourth position, hold one arm gently curving above your head and the other one out to the side. Put one foot exactly in front of the other with a little space between them.

5 Both arms are held above the head in fifth position to make a frame. The feet must be crossed and touching each other with the toes turned out to the side.

4th position

Anna is wearing special shoes called pointe *shoes to show the class how to stand with their feet in fourth and fifth position.*

5th position

Introducing the Barre

Now *it's time to* practise some exercises at the *barre*. Holding onto the wooden rails helps you to balance while you concentrate on your positions. To begin with you will learn how to stand at the *barre* and try simple exercises.

Pliés

Pliés, from the French word "plier" meaning "to bend", are one of the first movements you will learn and can be used in any of the five positions. To begin with you will learn a *demi plié*, or half knee bend. When you are older you can do a full knee bend, called a *grand plié*, shown here in fifth position.

April practises a demi plié, *in first position, keeping both heels on the ground.*

1 The pupils stand a little distance away from the barre *and* place both hands gently on it. Their elbows should be slightly lower than their hands.

French names

Ballet steps have French names because it was in France that ballet first became popular more than 300 years ago.

2 *Now they rise up gently on to demi-pointe, keeping their backs straight. This is called a rise.*

After learning to stand facing the barre, *the pupils turn to the side and hold the* barre *with one hand only.*

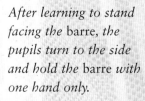

Balancing

The class are ready to come into the centre of the room now to try some balancing exercises without holding onto the *barre*. We use our balance all the time in everyday life when we walk, or run or perform any movement. But ballet dancers need to learn how to balance their bodies perfectly so that they can perform more difficult steps.

Wobbling

As Jamie practices a rise in the centre without the *barre* to hold onto it's hard not to wobble. It helps to fix your eyes on something straight ahead of you and keep looking at it.

The Dégagé

In this exercise you move your foot in a pointed position. As you do this you learn to transfer your weight slowly from one leg to another. Later on, this will help you to move quickly from one foot to the other.

| *1 Degagé* | *2 Degagé* | *3 Degagé* | *4 Degagé* |

1 To begin the *dégagé* stand with your feet in first position and hands on your shoulders. Keep your eyes looking straight ahead.

2 Now slide one foot out to the side with pointed toe. Try to really stretch the foot without moving your weight at the same time.

3 Put the heel of your stretched foot down on the floor and stand up tall. Your weight should now be between both legs.

4 Remember to move your weight over when you point the other foot and bring it back to stand in first position again.

Standing
on one leg

The class slowly lift one leg up high, to stand like a flamingo, with their hands on their hips to help them balance. Then they move their arms out to the side to grow even taller.

Skipping, Running and Marching

Jamie and her friends have done lots of running and skipping and marching in the playground, but in ballet you learn to do these movements in special ways. You learn how to run softly, find positions in the air, and move with expression and grace.

Coco keeps her back straight and her feet stretched downwards to give her skip lots of height.

Skipping

Moving from foot to foot, the position you make with your legs when you skip is the same as the one you made when standing on one leg like a flamingo. But this time you have to do it in the air. Point your toes, and keep one leg straight and the other one bent.

The girls stand in one corner holding their skirts out in preparation for running across the room.

Marching   **Clapping**

The boys learn to march up and down the room in time to the music, keeping their arms straight and feet stretched. Joe's right arm is stretched forward while his left leg is raised high. Clapping helps Alex to keep the rhythm of marching.

In ballet your movements should look light, delicate and skillful.

You can tell that Jamie, April and Coco are really enjoying themselves as they run lightly across the room on tiptoe.

April and Alex are inspired by a picture of older students leaping in the air. One day they may be strong enough to leap as high.

Leaping and Jumping

This part of the class is quick and lively and exciting. There are many kinds of jumps you will learn: fast jumps, travelling jumps or leaps, and jumps of different heights and shapes. But they must always look neat, controlled and graceful. And every jump must be well prepared so that you do not hurt yourself.

The class try the star shape on the floor.

Star shape on the floor

To practise the shape they will make in the air, the children first lie down on the floor and spread out their fingers and toes as wide as they can. They must remember to hold this shape in the air.

Joe remembers to stretch his hands and toes as he tries a star jump!

Ready to leap

It is important to prepare properly before you leap. Begin by bending the knees and then imagine you are a rocket about to take off, push down into the floor and spring into the air.

The boys really enjoy this energetic part of the class. As their muscles get stronger they will learn more complicated leaps.

Alex and Joe imagine that they are jumping over crocodiles. They will have to jump high if they don't want the crocodiles to bite them!

"This is my favourite part of the class. I can jump really high now."

Joe

Improvisation

The class stand around the piano and listen to the music carefully.

At *the end of* each class Anna lets the children make up their own dance. They begin by listening to the piano music. This helps them decide what sort of dance they are going to do. Is the music fast or slow? Should their dance be happy or sad? It's a time for the class to have fun, use their imaginations and dance their own story.

Using the space

The pupils spread out to give each other space. Sometimes on stage you will be dancing with lots of other dancers and your movements must be small and controlled. Other times you will have more room for bigger movements.

Expression

Dancers must tell their story without using words. Instead they use their bodies and movement to express themselves.

The pupils practise different facial expressions to tell the audience what they are feeling. The positions of the head, eyes and mouth all help convey feelings.

Scared

Sad

Angry

Free dance

When they are older, the children will perform in ballets where the stories are often well known and the steps are written down. But now they can invent their own stories and use their favourite steps.

Before they begin their dance, the girls help each other put on their tutus and tie pretty ribbons with a neat bow at the back.

Dressing up is a part of performing and the children enjoy wearing different clothes. This pretty white tutu helps April to feel and dance like a fairy princess.

Shy

Happy

A Dancing Day

A ballet class has so many different parts to it and there are so many things to learn! Some things you will find easy straight away and some things take more practice. You might like some parts better than others. But all the parts are important and part of a dancing day.

Artistic Fun Friendly

Warm-up: *the beginning of class is slow and gentle. Exercises to warm up your hands and arms and legs prepare you for more energetic movements later in the class.*

Posture: *sometimes exercises can be turned into fun games of pretend. Pretending to wear a crown helps you sit up straight.*

Partner work: *this part of the class gets a little faster as the children prepare to gallop across the room with a friend.*

Energetic Imaginative Appreciative

Jumping high: *for this part of the class you need lots of energy to jump and leap as high as you can now that your muscles are warm.*

Improvising: *now you can use your imagination to make up a dance of your own. You can put into practice all the new things you have learnt.*

Saying goodbye: *at the end of each class you line up to say goodbye and thank you to your teacher. You do this with a curtsey or bow.*

Pointe Shoes

Jamie helps Amy tie the pretty ribbons on her pointe shoes.

Jamie can't wait until she can wear *pointe* shoes. But she will have to! Your feet and legs need to be very strong to support your weight on your toes, probably when you are about eleven years old and have been learning ballet for several years. Even then, you will only wear *pointe* shoes for a short time at the end of each class. It will take several more years and lots of practice before you can actually start dancing on *pointe*.

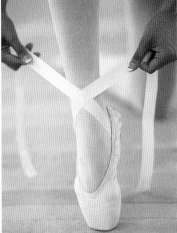

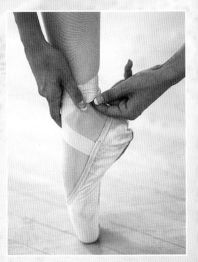

1 To tie the ribbons, begin by holding them halfway along their length and out to the side.

2 Now take the ribbons and cross them over the front of your foot so that they lie flat against your ankle.

3 The ribbons cross at the back and then tie together in a knot on the inside of your leg, just above the ankle.

4 Tuck in the ends of the ribbon under the knot so that it looks neat and tidy and feels comfortable.

Jamie imagines what it would be like to wear pointe shoes. Her teacher will tell her when she is strong enough. Then she must learn to look after her shoes and to sew on the ribbons herself.

Pointe shoes

Pointe shoes first became popular because wearing them made the ballerinas look so graceful. The hard tips of the shoes are made of layers of canvas and glue to support the toes and then covered in satin which wears out very quickly. Sometimes dancers wear out three pairs in just one performance.

5 The ribbons help support your ankles to keep them strong when you dance on *pointe*.

The pupils are really excited to be watching the older students. Anna wants them to enjoy themselves but also to learn from what they see.

Just Watch This!

The children have worked hard in class and today Anna decides they deserve a treat. It's their turn now to sit and watch while some of the older students in the school demonstrate what they have learnt and show the children what they will be able to do one day, if they train hard.

Joe is inspired by Martin's leap and wants to try too.

Joe tries to leap like Martin. He does very well but his muscles need to be stronger before he can jump as high.

Concentration

Remembering to keep your arms and fingers outstretched and your toes pointed while you are in the air is difficult. You must also be thinking ahead to when you land.

" *It's a great feeling when you're in the air but you have to concentrate all the time.* **"**

Martin

Martin makes this great leap, called a grand jeté, *look easy and for a moment it seems as though he is flying through the air, completely weightless.*

Preparation

Martin must be completely warmed up before he attempts any jumps. In particular he does exercises to strengthen his legs and feet muscles. The better the preparation, the better the jump.

Arabesque *on* pointe

Pas de Deux

After Martin's dazzling performance dancing on his own, Amy joins him to show the children how a boy and a girl dancing together can do things which one person dancing alone can't do, such as balancing for a long time and being lifted high in the air. This dancing partnership is called *pas de deux* and has some of the most beautiful and romantic movements in ballet.

Partners

Although ballet students only learn how to master the difficult movements of *pas de deux* from the age of 15 or 16, you will dance with a partner from the very beginning of your ballet classes. Both partners need to work hard. The girl has to develop strength to hold the positions and the boy will need to be strong enough to support and lift the girl.

Partners have to be good friends, ready to help and trust each other.

Arabesque

A dancer needs perfect balance to perform this beautiful movement where the arms and legs are stretched out to make long lines. Martin's position matches the line of Amy's position.

Martin is strong enough to lift Amy easily and hold her in this fish dive position. Amy must have total trust in him so she can concentrate on her position.

Jamie learns what it feels like to be lifted high on Martin's shoulders. It's a long way up but she's not scared because she knows Martin is holding her safely.

"*Anna showed us a costume from the ballet* Swan Lake*. It's black because it's worn by the nasty black swan, but it's still beautiful.*"

Coco

The children can hardly contain their excitement and burst into applause when Martin and Amy come back into the studio having changed into their beautiful costumes.

In Performance

For the final part of their demonstration, Martin and Amy put on their stage costumes and perform. Their costumes are beautiful but they must also be practical. The dancers have to be able to move freely in them and the audience should be able to see the movements they are making with their bodies.

Martin has to stand in exactly the right place so that he can support Amy without getting in the way of her movements.

Attitude derrière

This position is similar to an *arabesque*, but instead of making a long line shape, the raised leg makes a curved shape. The arm is held in fifth position.

Révérence

At the end of a class or a performance, the male dancers take low bows and the female dancers make deep, graceful curtseys to thank their teacher or the audience for their applause. This is called a *révérence*.

It is much
harder for
Martin to hold
Amy and to lift
her when she is
wearing her tutu.

At the end of their performance
Jamie is pleased to give Amy a
bouquet of flowers to show the
appreciation of the class.

Showtime!

The children get changed into their costumes, put their make-up on and get ready for their first performance.

*F*or *the last few months* the children have been practising hard to put on a performance of their own. They are all looking forward to showing everyone what they have learnt. When you first practise your dance on the stage you might feel shy but it is nice to hear the audience clapping at the end because they have really enjoyed watching you.

Jamie draws whiskers onto April's cheeks to make her look like a cat

Alex is dancing a fox dance.

Joe is a street urchin.

Character

The children each have a turn to dance on their own. They use their costumes in their dance; Alex twirling his tail and Joe his hat.

Make-up

Together with the costume, make-up is used in performance to transform you into a different character. Dancers learn how to put on their own make-up. They know that it has to be put on quite thickly so that it can be seen by the audience who may be sitting far away.

Costume

Wearing a costume is the most obvious way of telling the audience who or what you are trying to be. Sometimes the simplest costume can be the most effective. A long tail sewn onto a leotard and a hairband with ears on it instantly transform you into a cat.

Making yourself up to look different is fun and April enjoys it.

April the cat is about to pounce!

April suggests the movement of a cat with slow, stealthy steps.

41

Jamie's Dance

Some ballets tell stories, some ballets are about ideas or feelings and some ballets are meant just to show off the skill of the dancers. But all ballet, unlike other kinds of dance, is meant to be watched by an audience. When Jamie dances her dance of the fairy princess, she will be dancing not just for herself but also to give joy to her family and friends.

The happy princess

Jamie has put together the steps she has been taught in class to make a dance about a fairy princess. She spins and turns and jumps in the air, dancing gracefully and with feeling, just like a fairy princess.

The flowers

At the end, when she has finished her dance and the audience are clapping, Jamie feels really happy. She curtseys to the audience and this time it's *her* turn to be given a bouquet of flowers for putting on such a lovely performance and dancing so well!

Jennifer   April   Joe

Coco   Jamie   Alexei

"*Learning ballet is brilliant. I like it because my teacher is nice and I have made lots of friends and it's really fun.*"

April

Glossary

A

Arabesque – arab-ESK: a position where you stand on one leg with the other stretched out straight behind you.

Attitude derrière – at-ee-tewd dare-ee-AIR: a position where you stand on one leg with the other curved behind you.

B

Barre – bar: a wooden rail attached to the wall of the ballet studio to help you balance while you practise your exercises.

D

Dégagé – day-gar-SHAY: when you point your foot to the side, front or back in preparation for moving.

Demi plié – dem-EE plee-AY: a half-knee bend.

Demi pointe – dem-EE pointe: when you stand on the balls of your feet.

G

Grand jeté – gron she-TAY: a big, travelling jump with your legs stretched out in the air.

Grand plié – gron plee-AY: a full knee bend.

L

Leotard – the stretchy clothes worn by dancers.

P

Pas de deux – pah der DUH: two people dancing together.

Plié – plee-AY: bending your knees.

Posture – the way you stand or sit.

Pointe *shoes* – point: ballet shoes with ribbons and hard blocks at the toes worn by female dancers when their feet are strong enough after several years of training.

R

Relevé – re-lev-AY: the position where you rise up on tiptoe.

Révérence – rev-er-ONS: the curtsey or bow at the end of a class or a performance.

Rise – an exercise where you rise up to stand on the balls of your feet.

S

Studio – the room where you learn to dance.

T

Tutu – too-too: a costume with a frilly net skirt.

Index

Acknowledgements

Dorling Kindersley would like to thank the following for their help in the preparation and production of this book:

Central School of Ballet (Registered Charity No 285398), 10 Herbal Hill, Clerkenwell Road, London EC1R 5EG (www.centralschoolofballet.co.uk), for their kind permission to photograph the book there.

Special thanks to CSB Director Jane Hackett for acting as consultant and teacher Anna Berryman who was so good with the children; senior CSB students Martin Bell and Amy Grubb; junior CSB students Joe Cowley, Jennifer Griggs, April Gunawardena, Cosima Littlewood, Jamie-Rose Simpson and Alexei Winder; photographer David Handley; thanks also to Lisa Lanzarini and Catherine Saunders who were both absolutely wonderful at the photoshoot.